WOK

Simple and Delicious
WOK

Vicki Liley

APPLE

Contents

The Wok

The word *wok* simply means "cooking vessel" in Cantonese—an indication of how versatile and, indeed, indispensable this piece of equipment is for Asian cooks. Its shape, which has remained unchanged for centuries, was originally dictated by the Chinese stove. The stove had an opening in the top into which the round-bottomed wok securely fit.

A wok is a wonderful and practical addition to the contemporary kitchen. The shape accommodates small or large quantities of ingredients and allows control over how they are cooked. The large cooking surface evenly and efficiently conducts and holds heat. Although the wok is usually associated with stir-frying, there are few cooking methods for which it cannot be used and few ingredients that cannot be cooked in it, whether a recipe is Asian or Western in style.

Of the many woks available, all are basically bowl shaped with gently sloping sides. Some have looped handles on two sides; other have a long wooden handle on one side. Nonstick woks are easy to clean but may not promote browning of foods as thoroughly as those made of rolled or carbon steel. Other options include stainless steel woks and electric woks, which may not reach temperatures as high as those of cast iron or carbon steel.

Woks work best on gas stoves. A stand may be necessary to provide stability; the best choice is a stand with large perforations that promote good heat circulation. Flat-bottomed woks are suited for electric stove tops because they sit directly and securely on the heating element.

A wok with a diameter of 14 inches (35 cm) is a versatile size appropriate for the recipes in this book and for other dishes that yield four to six servings. A number of utensils go hand in hand with wok cooking: a lid, a bamboo steamer, a spatula and a slotted spoon.

Cooking in a Wok

BOILING A wok can serve as a saucepan, a frying pan and a stewing pot, suitable for simmering a delicate coconut sauce, boiling vegetables, simmering a soup or reducing a sauce.

STIR-FRYING This technique uses little fat and retains the fresh flavor, color and texture of ingredients. Meat, poultry, seafood, noodles and vegetables are cooked quickly; stirring them constantly helps ensure uniform doneness. The success of stir-frying depends on having all the ingredients ready before cooking starts.

BRAISING Meat or seafood can be browned to seal in the juices. Once liquid is added, the wok can be covered for slow simmering.

DEEP-FRYING The wok is ideal for deep-frying as it uses less oil than a deep fryer and can accommodate ingredients without crowding. Make sure the wok is secure on its stand or heating element before adding the oil. Pour oil into the wok and heat to 375°F (190°C) on a deep-frying thermometer or until a cube of bread sizzles and turns golden when dropped into hot oil.

STEAMING A bamboo steamer set over but not touching the water in a wok is ideal for cooking buns, dumplings, fish, vegetables and puddings. Half fill a wok with water (the steamer should not touch the water) and bring to a boil. Arrange the food in the steamer, cover, place the steamer in the wok and steam, adding more water to the wok when necessary. Lift steamer off the wok and carefully remove the food.

SEASONING A WOK Remove the thin coating of lacquer on woks of carbon steel or rolled steel by filling with cold water and 2 tablespoons of baking soda (bicarbonate of soda). Boil rapidly for 15 minutes. Drain and scrub off coating with a nylon pad. Repeat if any coating remains. Then rinse and dry the wok.

Carbon steel, rolled steel and cast iron woks need seasoning. Place the wok over low heat. When hot, carefully wipe with an oiled paper towel. Repeat with fresh towels until they wipe clean. Do not scrub the wok after cooking—use hot water and a sponge or nylon pad. Dry well and store in a dry, well-ventilated place. The oil may become rancid after a long period of time; the best way to prevent this is to use the wok often.

Appetizers and Entrées

Shrimp and avocado with wontons

Serves 4

GRAPEFRUIT DRESSING
¼ cup (2 fl oz/60 ml) grapefruit juice
¼ cup (2 fl oz/60 ml) olive oil
2 teaspoons palm sugar or brown sugar
1 tablespoon white wine vinegar
1 teaspoon peeled and grated fresh
   ginger
SALAD
3 cloves garlic, crushed

2 tablespoons vegetable oil, plus 3 cups
   (24 fl oz/750 ml) oil for deep-frying
20 jumbo shrimp (king prawns), peeled
   and deveined, tails intact
12 wonton wrappers
½ avocado, peeled, pitted and chopped
1 tomato, chopped
½ red onion, chopped
¼ cup (⅓ oz/10 g) chopped fresh
   cilantro (fresh coriander)

To make dressing, place grapefruit juice, olive oil, sugar, vinegar and ginger in screw-top jar. Shake well to combine and set aside.

To make salad, in wok over medium–high heat, warm 2 tablespoons vegetable oil. Add garlic and stir-fry until aromatic, about 1 minute. Raise heat to high, add shrimp and stir-fry until shrimp change color, 3–4 minutes. Remove from wok and drain on paper towels. Set aside to cool.

Heat 3 cups (24 fl oz/750 ml) oil in wok until it reaches 375°F (190°C) on deep-frying thermometer or until small bread cube dropped in oil sizzles and turns golden. Working in batches, add wonton wrappers and deep-fry until golden and crisp, about 1 minute. Using slotted spoon or tongs, remove from wok and drain on paper towels. Set aside to cool.

In bowl, combine avocado, tomato, onion and cilantro. Add shrimp and grapefruit dressing and gently stir until well combined. Cover and allow to stand for 10 minutes for flavors to develop.

Place one wonton on each plate and top with salad. Add another wonton and layer of salad. Top with third wonton. Serve immediately.

Peanut and chili bundles

Serves 8–10 as appetizer, 6 as entrée
1 cup (5½ oz/165 g) unsalted roasted peanuts
1 small red chili pepper, seeded and finely chopped
8 scallions (shallots/green onions), finely chopped
¼ cup (⅓ oz/10 g) chopped fresh cilantro (fresh coriander)
½ cup (4 fl oz/125 ml) lemon juice
½ cup (1 oz/30 g) fresh white bread crumbs
1 teaspoon superfine (caster) sugar
24 wonton wrappers
4 cups (32 fl oz/1 L) vegetable oil for deep-frying
lime wedges and Thai sweet chili sauce or soy sauce for serving

Place peanuts in food processor or blender and process until fine. Transfer to bowl. Add chili pepper, scallions, cilantro, lemon juice, bread crumbs and sugar. Mix well.

Place wonton wrappers on work surface and cover with damp towel to prevent them from drying out. Working with one wrapper at a time, place 1 teaspoon peanut filling in middle. Brush edges with water, gather edges together and twist

to seal. Set aside, covered with plastic wrap. Repeat with remaining wonton wrappers.

Heat oil in wok until it reaches 375°F (190°C) on deep-frying thermometer or until small bread cube cropped in oil sizzles and turns golden. Working in batches, add wontons and fry until golden, 1–2 minutes. Using slotted spoon, remove from wok and drain on paper towels.

Serve bundles hot with lime wedges and with Thai sweet chili sauce or soy sauce for dipping.

Steamed shrimp dumplings

Serves 6 as appetizer, 3 or 4 as entrée
8 oz (250 g) jumbo shrimp (king prawns), peeled and deveined
2 tablespoons finely chopped drained canned water chestnuts
2 scallions (shallots/spring onions), chopped, plus shredded scallions for serving
1 tablespoon light soy sauce, plus soy sauce for dipping
½ teaspoon Asian sesame oil
12 wonton wrappers

Place shrimp in food processor and process until smooth. Transfer to bowl. Add water chestnuts, chopped scallions, 1 tablespoon soy sauce and sesame oil. Mix until well combined. Place wonton wrappers on work surface and cover with damp kitchen towel to prevent them from drying out. Working with one wrapper at a time, lay it on work surface and place 1 teaspoon shrimp filling in middle. Brush edges with water, gather edges together and twist to seal. Set aside, covered with plastic wrap. Repeat with remaining wonton wrappers.

Line bamboo steamer with parchment (baking) paper. Half fill wok with water (steamer should not touch water) and bring water to boil. Arrange filled wontons in steamer, cover and place steamer over boiling water. Steam for 20 minutes, adding more water to wok when necessary. Lift steamer off wok and carefully remove dumplings from steamer.

Arrange dumplings on individual plates and garnish with shredded scallions. Serve warm with soy sauce for dipping.

Mini crab spring rolls

Serves 6–8 as appetizer,
3–4 as entrée

DIPPING SAUCE

1 tablespoon fish sauce
3 tablespoons lime juice
1 scallion (shallot/spring onion),
    finely chopped
1 small red chili pepper, seeded
    and chopped
1 teaspoon palm sugar or brown sugar
1 tablespoon finely chopped fresh
    cilantro (fresh coriander)
1 tablespoon rice wine vinegar
½ small cucumber, peeled, seeded
    and finely chopped

CRAB SPRING ROLLS

2 teaspoons vegetable oil, plus 4 cups
    (32 fl oz/1 L) oil for deep-frying
1 bunch bok choy, trimmed
    and shredded
4 kaffir lime leaves, finely shredded,
    or 1 teaspoon grated lime zest
8 oz (250 g) fresh or drained
    canned crabmeat
2 tablespoons chopped fresh
    cilantro (fresh coriander)
1 tablespoon lime juice
18–20 thawed frozen mini spring roll
    wrappers, about 4½-in (11.5-cm)
    square
2 teaspoons cornstarch (cornflour)
    mixed with 2 tablespoons water

To make dipping sauce, combine fish sauce, lime juice, scallion, chili pepper, sugar, cilantro, vinegar and cucumber. Stir to combine; set aside. To make spring rolls, in wok over high heat, warm 2 teaspoons vegetable oil. Add bok choy and stir-fry until softened, about 1 minute. Remove from heat, place in bowl and allow to cool completely. Stir in kaffir lime leaves, crabmeat, cilantro and lime juice. Mix until well combined.

Separate spring roll wrappers, place on work surface and cover with damp kitchen towel to prevent them from drying out. Working with one wrapper at a time, place 1 tablespoon filling in middle. Using fingertips, moisten edges with cornstarch and water mixture. Roll up diagonally to enclose filling, tucking in edges. Seal with cornstarch and water mixture. Cover with plastic wrap; set aside. Repeat with rest of wrappers.

Heat 4 cups (32 fl oz/1 L) vegetable oil in wok until it reaches 375°F (190°C) on deep-frying thermometer or until a small bread cube dropped in oil sizzles and turns golden. Working in batches, fry rolls until golden, about 1 minute. Using a slotted spoon, remove rolls and drain on paper towels. Serve hot with dipping sauce.

Cilantro shrimp toasts

Serves 10–12 as appetizer

1 lb (500 g) jumbo shrimp (king prawns), peeled and deveined

4 French shallots, coarsely chopped

1 lemongrass stalk, bruised and coarsely chopped

2 cloves garlic

1 egg white

2 teaspoons fish sauce

1 teaspoon lemon juice

1 small red chili pepper, seeded and chopped

4 kaffir lime leaves, shredded, or 1 teaspoon grated lime zest

2 tablespoons finely chopped fresh cilantro (fresh coriander)

35–40 slices white bread

2 tablespoons sesame seeds

3 cups (24 fl oz/750 ml) vegetable oil for deep-frying

Place shrimp, shallots, lemongrass, garlic, egg white, fish sauce, lemon juice and chili pepper in food processor and process until smooth. Transfer to bowl. Stir in kaffir lime leaves or lime zest and cilantro. Mix until well combined.

Using star-shaped or round cookie cutter 3 inches (7.5 cm) in diameter, cut one star or round from each bread slice (reserve leftover bread for making

crumbs). Spread 1 scant teaspoon shrimp mixture on each bread shape. Sprinkle with sesame seeds and press gently into shrimp mixture.

Heat oil in large wok until it reaches 375°F (190°C) on deep-frying thermometer or until small bread cube dropped in oil sizzles and turns golden. Working in batches, add toasts and fry until golden on both sides, 1–2 minutes. Using slotted spoon, remove from wok and drain on paper towels.

Arrange toasts on serving platter or individual plates and serve hot.

Fried chicken wontons

Serves 10–12 as appetizer,
6–8 as entrée
1 tablespoon vegetable oil, plus 4 cups
   (32 fl oz/1 L) oil for deep-frying
1 onion, chopped
1 clove garlic, crushed
8 oz (250 g) ground (minced) chicken

2 tablespoon chunky peanut butter
1 tablespoon Thai sweet chili sauce
1 tablespoon lemon juice
¼ cup (⅓ oz/10 g) chopped fresh
   cilantro (fresh coriander)
48 round wonton wrappers
chili oil for serving

In wok over medium–high heat, warm
1 tablespoon vegetable oil. Add onion
and garlic and stir-fry until softened,
1–2 minutes. Add chicken and stir-fry
until chicken changes color. Remove
from heat. Add peanut butter, chili
sauce, lemon juice and cilantro. Allow
to cool completely.

Place wonton wrappers on work
surface and cover with damp kitchen
towel to prevent them from drying
out. Working with one wrapper at a
time, lay it on work surface and place
1 heaping teaspoon chicken filling in
middle. Brush edges with water. Place
another wonton wrapper on top and
firmly press edges together. Set aside, covered with plastic wrap. Repeat with
remaining wonton wrappers.

Heat 4 cups (32 fl oz/1 L) vegetable oil in large wok until it reaches 375°F
(190°C) on deep-frying thermometer or until small bread cube dropped in oil
sizzles and turns golden. Working in batches, add wontons and fry until golden
on both sides, 1–2 minutes. Using a slotted spoon, remove from wok and drain
on paper towels.

Serve wontons hot, accompanied with chili oil.

Soups

Coconut and vegetable soup

Serves 4

1 tablespoon vegetable oil

¼ teaspoon shrimp paste

1 clove garlic, crushed

¼ cup (⅓ oz/10 g) chopped fresh cilantro (fresh coriander) stems

4 scallions (shallots/green onions) chopped

3 cups (24 fl oz/750 ml) chicken or vegetable broth

1 cup (8 fl oz/250 ml) coconut milk

1 tablespoon fish sauce

2 cups (6 oz/180 g) finely shredded green cabbage

12 snow peas (mange-touts), trimmed and sliced crosswise

1 carrot, peeled and julienned

1 cup (3 oz/90 g) small broccoli florets

3 tablespoons lime juice

2 teaspoons sambal oelek

1 tablespoon chopped fresh cilantro (fresh coriander)

In wok over medium heat, warm oil. Add shrimp paste, garlic, cilantro stems and scallions and stir-fry until softened, about 1 minute. Add broth, coconut milk and fish sauce. Bring to boil, then reduce heat to low. Add cabbage, snow peas, carrot and broccoli. Simmer, uncovered, until vegetables are just tender, about 10 minutes.

Stir in lime juice, sambal oelek and cilantro.

Serve hot, ladled into individual bowls.

Carrot, coconut and ginger soup

Serves 4

1 tablespoon vegetable oil

1 teaspoon Asian sesame oil

1 small red chili pepper, seeded and
  chopped

4 cloves garlic, crushed

3 teaspoons peeled and grated fresh
  ginger

2 onions, chopped

2 lb (1 kg) carrots, peeled and sliced

1 teaspoon ground cumin

1 teaspoon ground turmeric

4 cups (32 fl oz/1 L) coconut milk

2 cups (16 fl oz/500 ml) vegetable or
  chicken broth

salt and ground pepper to taste

fresh tarragon leaves for serving

In wok over medium heat, warm vegetable and sesame oils. Add chili pepper, garlic and ginger and stir-fry until aromatic, about 1 minute. Add onions, carrots, cumin and turmeric and stir-fry until onions are softened, about 2 minutes.

Pour in coconut milk and broth. Bring to boil, reduce heat to low and simmer, uncovered, until carrots are tender, 12–15 minutes. Remove from heat.

Working in batches, ladle soup into food processor or blender and process until smooth. Return to wok and heat through for 2 minutes. Taste and season with salt and pepper.

To serve, ladle into individual bowls and garnish with tarragon leaves.

Miso with scallops and ginger

Serves 4
8 oz (250 g) scallops, cut in half if large
¼ cup (1 oz/30 g) peeled and shredded fresh ginger
¼ cup (⅓ oz/10 g) chopped fresh cilantro (fresh coriander)
1½ cups (12 fl oz/375 ml) water
1 lemongrass stalk, bruised and finely chopped
4 kaffir lime leaves, finely shredded, or 1 teaspoon grated lime zest
2 tablespoons red miso paste
1 teaspoon lime juice

Place scallops, ginger, cilantro, water and lemongrass in wok. Bring to boil. Reduce heat, cover and simmer until scallops are opaque, 1–2 minutes.

Remove from heat and pour through strainer into bowl. Reserve liquid. Set scallops and spices aside and keep warm.

Measure liquid and add water to make 4 cups (32 fl oz/1 L). Return to wok and bring to boil. Stir in miso and lime juice, reduce heat and simmer for 3 minutes.

To serve, divide scallops among individual plates, and ladle miso into small bowls.

Chicken broth with dumplings

Serves 4

2 tablespoons butter, softened

1 egg, beaten

1 cup (2 oz/60 g) fresh white
bread crumbs

2 teaspoons peeled and grated fresh
ginger, plus 3 thin slices ginger

2 tablespoons chopped fresh
cilantro (fresh coriander)

4 cups (32 fl oz/1 L) chicken broth

2 lemongrass stalks, bruised
and chopped

1 small red chili pepper, seeded
and chopped

¼ cup (1 oz/30 g) shredded scallions
(shallots/green onions)

In bowl, combine butter, egg, bread crumbs, grated ginger and cilantro. Using wooden spoon or fingertips, mix until well combined. Set dumpling mixture aside.

Place chicken broth, ginger slices, lemongrass and chili pepper in large wok. Bring to boil, reduce heat to low and simmer, uncovered, for 10 minutes. Strain through fine-mesh strainer into bowl. Discard solids. Return broth to wok and keep warm.

Place 3 cups (24 fl oz/750 ml) water into another wok or saucepan. Bring to boil and reduce heat so water gently simmers. Working in batches, drop 1 heaping teaspoon dumpling mixture, into simmering water. Cook until firm, 2–3 minutes. Using slotted spoon, remove from simmering water. Repeat with remaining mixture.

Ladle hot broth into individual bowls. Divide dumplings among bowls and garnish with shredded scallions. Serve immediately.

Mushroom and chicken soup

Serves 4

4 Chinese dried mushrooms
4 cups (32 fl oz/1 L) chicken broth
2 cloves garlic, crushed
1 teaspoon peeled and grated ginger
1 tablespoon rice vinegar
2 teaspoons palm sugar or brown sugar
1 chicken fillet, about 5 oz (150 g), thinly sliced
6 scallions (shallots/spring onions), chopped
2 lemongrass stalks, bruised and sliced
1 small red chili pepper, seeded and chopped

Place mushrooms in small bowl, add boiling water to cover and allow to stand until softened, 10–15 minutes. Drain and squeeze excess liquid from mushrooms. Thinly slice, discarding thick stems.

Place broth, garlic, ginger, vinegar and sugar in wok. Bring to boil, reduce heat to low and simmer, uncovered, for 5 minutes. Stir in sliced mushrooms, chicken, scallions, lemongrass and chili pepper. Simmer until chicken is opaque, about 15 minutes. Serve hot, ladled into bowls.

Rice and Noodles

Nasi goreng

Serves 4–6

3 teaspoons peeled and grated
   fresh ginger
1 teaspoon ground turmeric
1 teaspoon shrimp paste
2 teaspoons chili sauce
3 tablespoons peanut oil
1 onion, chopped
3 cloves garlic, crushed
½ red bell pepper (capsicum), seeded
   and chopped
1 celery stalk, chopped
1 carrot, peeled and chopped

½ cup (2½ oz/75 g) thawed
   frozen peas
4 oz (125 g) Chinese barbecue
   pork, chopped
1 cup (4 oz/125 g) fresh bean
   sprouts, rinsed
1 cup (3 oz/90 g) shredded bok choy
4 cups (20 oz/625 g) cold cooked
   jasmine rice
4 oz (125 g) cooked shrimp (prawns),
   peeled and deveined, tails intact
¼ cup (2 fl oz/60 ml) coconut milk
2 tablespoons light soy sauce

Combine ginger, turmeric, shrimp paste and chili sauce in small bowl. Mix to form paste. Set aside.

In wok over medium–high heat, warm peanut oil. Add onion and garlic and stir-fry until onion softens, about 1 minute. Stir in spice paste, bell pepper, celery, carrot, peas, pork, bean sprouts and bok choy. Raise heat to high and stir-fry until vegetables soften slightly, 3–4 minutes. Add rice and shrimp and stir-fry until rice is heated through, about 3 minutes. Combine coconut milk and soy sauce, add to wok and stir until evenly combined and mixture is hot.

Spoon into individual bowls. Serve hot as main course or as accompaniment to other stir-fried dishes.

Chili fried rice

Serves 4

3 tablespoons vegetable oil

1 onion, chopped

1 small red chili pepper, seeded and
chopped

1 tablespoon red curry paste

5 oz (150 g) pork fillet, thinly sliced

12 jumbo shrimp (king prawns), peeled
and deveined, tails intact

4 cups (20 oz/625 g) cooked white
rice, chilled

2 eggs, beaten

1 tablespoon fish sauce

½ cup (1½ oz/45 g) chopped scallions
(shallots/spring onions)

⅓ cup (½ oz/15 g) chopped fresh
cilantro (fresh coriander)

3 small red chili flowers (optional)

In wok over medium–high heat, warm oil. Add onion and chili pepper and stir-fry until onion is softened, about 2 minutes. Stir in curry paste and cook for 1 minute. Add pork and stir-fry until pork changes color, 3–4 minutes. Add shrimp and stir-fry until shrimp change color, about 3 minutes. Add rice and

stir-fry until rice is coated with oil. Push rice to one side of wok. Add beaten eggs and allow to partially set without stirring, them mix with rice. Stir in fish sauce, scallions and cilantro.

Serve hot as main course or as accompaniment to stir-fried dishes. Garnish with chili flowers, if desired.

NOTE To make red chili flower, using sharp knife, make closely spaced cuts along the length of small red chili pepper, allowing chili to stay attached at stem end. Place in bowl of ice water. Chill until chili curls, about 15 minutes.

Fried noodles with pork

Serves 4

8 oz (250 g) fresh or dried egg noodles
1 tablespoon vegetable oil
1 bunch Chinese broccoli, cut into 3-in (7.5-cm) lengths
8 oz (250 g) Chinese barbecue pork, sliced
½ cup (5 oz/150 g) chunky peanut butter
2 teaspoon Asian sesame oil
2 tablespoons light soy sauce
2 teaspoons garam masala
3 cloves garlic, crushed
1 small red chili pepper, seeded and chopped

Bring saucepan of water to boil. Add noodles and cook until tender, about 3 minutes for fresh noodles, about 5 minutes for dried noodles. (If using precooked noodles, soak in boiling water for 8–10 minutes.) Drain and keep warm.

In wok over medium–high heat, warm vegetable oil. Add broccoli and pork and stir-fry for 4 minutes. In small bowl, combine peanut butter, sesame oil, soy sauce, garam masala, garlic and chili. Mix until well combined. Add peanut butter mixture and noodles to wok. Raise heat to high and stir-fry until heated through, about 1 minute. Do not overcook.

Serve hot.

Salmon laksa

Serves 6

6½ oz (200 g) cellophane (bean thread) noodles

3 small red chili peppers, seeded and chopped

3 cloves garlic

1 piece peeled fresh ginger, about 2½ in (6 cm) long

½ cup (⅔ oz/20 g) fresh cilantro (fresh coriander) leaves

3 teaspoons vegetable oil

1 teaspoon Asian sesame oil

4 cups (32 fl oz/1 L) coconut milk

3 cups (24 fl oz/750 ml) fish broth or 1½ cups (12 fl oz/375 ml) each clam juice and water

8 oz (250 g) salmon fillet, skin and errant bones removed, sliced into 12 thin slices

2 tablespoons lemon juice

1 tablespoon fish sauce

4 scallions (shallots/spring onions), sliced

¼ cup (¼ oz/7 g) fresh mint leaves

Place noodles in bowl and soak in boiling water for 10 minutes. Drain and set aside. Place chili peppers, garlic, ginger and cilantro in food processor. Process to form smooth paste.

In wok over medium–high heat, warm vegetable and sesame oils. Add spice paste and cook until aromatic, about 1 minute. Add coconut milk and broth or clam juice and water, and bring to boil. Reduce heat to low and simmer, uncovered, for 10 minutes. Add salmon, lemon juice and fish sauce and simmer until salmon is opaque, 2–3 minutes.

To serve, divide noodles among individual bowls. Ladle soup over noodles. Sprinkle each serving with scallions and mint leaves.

Noodles with baked vegetables

Serves 4

8 oz (250 g) fresh or dried egg
   noodles or udon noodles
1 lb (500 g) butternut squash
   (pumpkin), cut into 1-in (2.5-cm)
   pieces
2 carrots, peeled and cut into
   1-in (2.5-cm) pieces
3 tablespoons vegetable oil
5 cloves garlic, crushed

6½ oz (200 g) zucchini (courgette),
   cut into 1-in (2.5-cm) pieces
2 onions, chopped
1 cup (8 fl oz/250 ml) coconut milk
¼ cup (⅓ oz/10 g) chopped fresh
   cilantro (fresh coriander)
1 small red chili pepper, seeded
   and chopped
salt and ground pepper to taste

Preheat oven to 400°F (200°C/Gas 6). Bring saucepan of water to boil. Add
noodles and cook until tender, about 2½ minutes for fresh udon noodles,
about 3 minutes for fresh egg noodles, about 5 minutes for dried egg noodles,
10–12 minutes for dried udon noodles. Drain and set aside.

   In baking dish, combine squash, carrots, 2 tablespoons vegetable oil and
3 cloves garlic. Toss to coat vegetables in oil. Bake, uncovered, for 15 minutes.
Remove from oven, add zucchini, stir vegetables, return to oven and bake until
vegetables are tender, about 15 minutes.

In wok over medium–high heat,
warm remaining 1 tablespoon
vegetable oil. Add onions and
remaining 2 cloves garlic and stir-fry
until onions soften, 2–3 minutes.
Add coconut milk, cilantro and chili
pepper. Stir until heated through,
3–4 minutes. Add baked vegetables
and noodles. Cook until heated
through, 1–2 minutes. Taste and
season with salt and pepper.

   Divide among individual bowls and
serve immediately.

Ginger-coconut rice

Serves 4–6
2 tablespoons vegetable oil
1 teaspoon chili oil
1 onion, chopped
1 red bell pepper (capsicum), seeded and chopped
3 cloves garlic, crushed
3 teaspoons peeled and grated fresh ginger
1½ cups (10½ oz/330 g) short-grain white rice
1½ cups (12 fl oz/375 ml) chicken broth
1 cup (8 fl oz/250 ml) water
½ cup (4 fl oz/125 ml) coconut milk
3 scallions (shallots/spring onions)
3 tablespoons chopped fresh cilantro (fresh coriander)
2 tablespoons unsweetened shredded coconut, toasted
3 tablespoons lemon juice
¼ cup (1 oz/30 g) unsweetened shredded coconut for serving

In wok over medium–high heat, warm vegetable and chili oils. Add onion, bell pepper, garlic and ginger and stir-fry until softened, about 3 minutes. Add rice and stir until well coated with oil, about 2 minutes.

Add broth, water and coconut milk and bring to boil. Reduce heat to low, cover and simmer until all liquid is absorbed and rice is tender, 15–20 minutes. Remove from heat and stir in scallions, cilantro, toasted coconut and lemon juice. Serve hot, topped with shredded coconut.

Seafood

Shrimp in ginger-coconut sauce

Serves 4

2 tablespoons peeled and grated fresh ginger
4 cloves garlic, crushed
1 tablespoon ground turmeric
1 small red chili pepper, seeded and chopped
2 tablespoons white vinegar
2 tablespoons peanut oil
2 onions, chopped
1 lb (500 g) jumbo shrimp (king prawns), peeled and deveined, tails intact
2 tomatoes, chopped
¾ cup (6 fl oz/180 ml) coconut milk
2 teaspoons cracked black pepper
2 tablespoons chopped fresh cilantro (fresh coriander)
¼ cup (¼ oz/7 g) small whole cilantro (coriander leaves)

Place ginger, garlic, turmeric, chili pepper and vinegar in food processor or blender. Process to form paste.

In wok over medium–high heat, warm peanut oil. Add onions and spice paste and stir-fry until onions soften, 2–3 minutes. Add shrimp and stir-fry until shrimp change color, 3–4 minutes. Stir in tomatoes and cook until soft, about 2 minutes. Add coconut milk, reduce heat to low, cover and simmer until sauce thickens slightly and shrimp are tender, 6–8 minutes. Stir in pepper and chopped cilantro. Serve hot, garnished with cilantro leaves.

Stir-fried octopus with long beans and snow peas

Serves 4
1 lb (500 g) baby octopus
1 tablespoon light soy sauce
3 tablespoons vegetable oil
1 tablespoon dry sherry
2 cloves garlic, crushed
2 teaspoons grated lime zest
2 tablespoons lime juice

3 small red chili peppers, seeded and halved
5 oz (150 g) long beans, cut into 4-in (10-cm) lengths
4 kaffir lime leaves, shredded, or 1 teaspoon grated lime zest
5 oz (155 g) snow peas (mange-touts), trimmed and sliced crosswise

Working with one octopus at a time, slit open head and remove intestines. Rinse and place in glass or ceramic bowl. In small bowl, combine soy sauce, 1 tablespoon vegetable oil, sherry, garlic, 2 teaspoons lime zest and lime juice. Pour over octopus, cover and refrigerate for 1 hour.

Drain octopus and reserve marinade. In wok over medium heat, warm remaining 2 tablespoons vegetable oil. Add chili peppers and stir-fry until aromatic, 1–2 minutes. Add octopus and stir-fry for 2 minutes. Add beans, lime leaves or lime zest, snow peas and reserved marinade. Stir-fry until vegetables are tender-crisp and octopus is cooked through (do not overcook or octopus will toughen), 1–2 minutes. Serve hot.

Spicy snapper with parsnip chips

Serves 4

2 teaspoon ground cumin

1 green chili pepper, seeded and sliced

½ cup (⅔ oz/20 g) fresh cilantro (fresh coriander) leaves

3 cloves garlic

1 piece peeled fresh ginger, about 1¼ in (3 cm)

2 teaspoons garam marsala

4 small snapper, 6–8 oz (180–250 g) each, cleaned

6 cups (48 fl oz/1.5 L) vegetable oil for deep-frying

2 parsnips, peeled

lime wedges for serving

Place cumin, chili pepper, cilantro, garlic, ginger and garam marsala in food processor and process until smooth. Using sharp knife, cut 3 shallow slits in each side of fish. Rub spice mixture into each side. Place on glass or ceramic plate, cover and refrigerate for 1 hour.

Heat vegetable oil in wok until it reaches 375°F (190°C) on deep-frying thermometer or until small bread cube dropped in oil sizzles and turns golden.

Add fish, one at a time, and cook, turning once, until golden and crisp on both sides, about 4 minutes. Using tongs and spatula, carefully remove fish from wok and drain on paper towels. Repeat with remaining fish. Keep warm.

Thinly slice parsnips lengthwise, using vegetable peeler. Add slices to wok and cook until golden and crisp, about 1 minute. Using slotted spoon, remove from wok and drain on paper towels.

Arrange fish and parsnip chips on individual plates. Garnish with lime wedge and serve.

Scallops with arugula pesto and sweet potato purée

Serves 4

ARUGULA PESTO
1 bunch arugula (rocket)
¼ cup (1 oz/30 g) pine nuts, toasted
¼ cup (1 oz/30 g) grated parmesan
   cheese
ground pepper to taste
2 cloves garlic, crushed
¼ cup (2 fl oz/60 ml) extra virgin
   olive oil

SCALLOPS AND SWEET POTATO PURÉE
1 lb (500 g) sweet potatoes, peeled and
   cut into 2-in (5-cm) pieces
2 tablespoons olive oil
3 cloves garlic, crushed
2 tablespoons vegetable oil
1 small red chili pepper, seeded and
   chopped
1 lb (500 g) scallops, halved if large
1 tablespoon lime juice
lime wedges for serving

To make pesto, place arugula, pine nuts, parmesan cheese, pepper and garlic in food processor. Process until finely chopped. With motor running, gradually pour in olive oil and process until well combined. Set aside.

Half fill saucepan with water. Bring to boil, add sweet potatoes, reduce heat to medium and cook until tender, 10–12 minutes. Drain, transfer to bowl and mash with fork or potato masher. Stir in olive oil and 2 garlic cloves. Set aside and keep warm.

In wok over medium heat, warm vegetable oil. Add chili pepper and remaining garlic clove and stir-fry until aromatic, about 1 minute. Add scallops and stir-fry until tender (do not overcook or scallops will toughen), 2–3 minutes. Remove from heat and stir in lime juice.

To serve, spoon sweet potato purée on individual plates. Top with pesto, then place scallops on pesto. Serve hot, accompanied with lime wedges. Store any leftover pesto in screw-top jar in refrigerator.

Beef and Pork

Beef stir-fry with Chinese greens

Serves 4

10½ oz (315 g) sirloin (rump) or round (topside) steak
3 tablespoons vegetable oil
4 cloves garlic, crushed
1 tablespoon peeled and grated fresh ginger
2 small red chili peppers, seeded and chopped
1 bunch Chinese broccoli or 6 celery stalks, trimmed
and cut into 1¼-in (3-cm) lengths
7 oz (220 g) sugar snap peas or snow peas (mange-touts), trimmed
3½ oz (105 g) fresh bean sprouts, rinsed
1 tablespoon oyster sauce
1 teaspoon sambal oelek
steamed white rice for serving

Enclose steak in freezer wrap and freeze until slightly firm, about 30 minutes.
Remove from freezer and thinly slice. In bowl, combine beef, 1 tablespoon
vegetable oil, garlic and ginger. Cover and refrigerate for 30 minutes.

Drain beef from marinade, discarding marinade. In wok over medium–high
heat, warm remaining 2 tablespoons vegetable oil. Working in batches, add beef
and stir-fry until brown, 1–2 minutes. Remove from wok and drain on paper
towels. Add chili pepper, broccoli or celery, sugar snap peas or snow peas and
bean sprouts and stir-fry until tender-crisp, 2–3 minutes. Add beef, oyster sauce
and sambal oelek. Stir-fry until heated through, about 1 minute.

Serve hot, accompanied with steamed white rice.

Red curry beef

Serves 4
**8 oz (250 g) sirloin (rump) or round (topside) steak
1 tablespoon vegetable oil
1 tablespoon red curry paste
1 cup (8 fl oz/250 ml) coconut milk
2 teaspoons fish sauce
1 teaspoon palm sugar or brown sugar
1 cup (6 oz/180 g) drained canned baby corn
⅓ cup (2 oz/60 g) drained canned straw mushrooms
½ cup (½ oz/15 g) small fresh basil leaves
steamed white rice for serving**

Enclose steak in freezer wrap and freeze until slightly firm, about 30 minutes. Remove from freezer and thinly slice. In wok over medium–high heat, warm oil. Working in batches, add beef and stir-fry until brown, 1–2 minutes. Remove from wok and drain on paper towels. Add curry paste to wok and cook until paste bubbles, 10–15 seconds. Stir in coconut milk, fish sauce, sugar, corn and mushrooms. Bring to boil, reduce heat and simmer, uncovered, for 5 minutes. Add beef and stir-fry until heated through, about 1 minute.

Spoon into bowls and sprinkle each serving with basil leaves. Serve hot, accompanied with steamed white rice.

Dry beef curry with sweet potato

Serves 4

1 onion, chopped

2 cloves garlic

1 teaspoon shrimp paste

1 teaspoon ground cumin

2 teaspoons ground cilantro (coriander)

1 tablespoon chopped lemongrass

½ teaspoon ground turmeric

1 teaspoon ground paprika

1 teaspoon grated lime zest

2 tablespoons vegetable oil

11 oz (330 g) sirloin (rump)
or round (topside) steak, cut into
1¼-in (3-cm) cubes

1 cup (8 fl oz/250 ml) water

7 oz (220 g) sweet potato, peeled
and finely diced

1 long red chili pepper, seeded
and sliced

1 long green chili pepper, seeded
and sliced

steamed white rice for serving

Place onion, garlic, shrimp paste, cumin, coriander, lemongrass, turmeric, paprika and lime zest in food processor. Process until smooth. Set aside.

In wok over medium–high heat, warm vegetable oil. Working in batches, add beef and stir-fry until brown, 3–4 minutes. Remove from wok and drain on paper

towels. Add spice blend to wok and cook until aromatic, about 1 minute.

Add beef and water and bring to boil. Reduce heat to low, cover and simmer, stirring occasionally, for 30 minutes. Stir in sweet potato and simmer, uncovered, until sweet potato is tender, about 10 minutes. (Add a little more water if necessary.)

To serve, spoon into bowls, and sprinkle with sliced chili peppers. Accompany with steamed white rice.

Pork and nectarine stir-fry

Serves 4–6
2 tablespoons vegetable oil
3 cloves garlic, crushed
1 small red chili pepper, seeded and chopped
1 lb (500 g) pork fillet, thinly sliced
1 bunch choy sum or spinach, trimmed and cut into 1¼-in (3-cm) lengths
3 kaffir lime leaves, shredded
2½ tablespoons light soy sauce
2 teaspoons lime juice
2 firm nectarines, pitted and sliced
steamed white rice for serving

In wok over medium–high heat, warm vegetable oil. Add garlic and chili pepper and stir-fry until aromatic, about 1 minute. Add pork, choy sum or spinach and lime leaves and stir-fry until pork changes color, 3–4 minutes. Add soy sauce, lime juice and nectarines and stir-fry until heated through, 1–2 minutes.

Serve hot, accompanied with steamed white rice.

Fried pork in endive

Serves 4

1 tablespoon vegetable oil

2 cloves garlic, crushed

1 tablespoon peeled and grated
  fresh ginger

6 scallions (shallots/spring onions),
  chopped

½ teaspoon shrimp paste

1 tablespoon chopped lemongrass

2 teaspoons sambal oelek

7 oz (220 g) pork fillet, finely chopped

8 oz (250 g) cherry tomatoes, quartered

1 tablespoon coconut milk

3 tablespoons chopped fresh cilantro
  (fresh coriander)

3 heads Belgian endive
  (chicory/witloof), cored and
  leaves separated

In wok over medium heat, warm vegetable oil. Add garlic, ginger, scallions, shrimp paste, lemongrass and sambal oelek and stir-fry until aromatic, about 2 minutes. Add pork and cook until pork changes color, about 3 minutes.

Stir in tomatoes and coconut milk and stir-fry until tomatoes soften slightly, 1–2 minutes. Remove from heat and stir in cilantro. To serve, spoon pork filling into endive leaves. Divide among individual plates and serve hot.

Pork and lime patties

Serves 4

8 oz (250 g) ground (minced) pork
2 teaspoons fish sauce
1 teaspoon oyster sauce ·
2 teaspoons sambal oelek
1 egg white, lightly beaten
2 cloves garlic, crushed
2 tablespoons cornstarch (cornflour)

2 teaspoon grated lime zest
4 kaffir lime leaves, shredded
¼ cup (1 oz/30 g) chopped scallions
   (shallots/spring onions)
½ cup (4 fl oz/125 ml) vegetable oil
   for frying
Thai sweet chili sauce for serving

In bowl, combine pork, fish sauce, oyster sauce, sambal oelek and egg white.
Mix well. Add garlic, cornstarch, lime zest, lime leaves and scallions. Using
moistened hands, mix until well combined. Divide mixture into 16 pieces and
shape into patties.

In wok over medium heat, warm vegetable oil. Working in batches, add
pork patties and fry, turning once, until tender and golden on both sides,
6–8 minutes. Drain on paper towels. Serve hot with Thai sweet chili sauce.

Chicken and Duck

Chicken chow mein

Serves 4

6 cups (48 fl oz/1.5 L) vegetable oil for deep-frying, plus 2 tablespoons oil
6½ oz (200 g) fresh thin egg noodles
3 cloves garlic, crushed
1 tablespoon peeled and grated fresh ginger
1 onion, cut into eighths
1 lb (500 g) skinless chicken thigh fillets, cut into ¾-in (2-cm) cubes
1 red bell pepper (capsicum), seeded and sliced
1 green bell pepper (capsicum), seeded and sliced
1 bunch choy sum or spinach, trimmed and cut into 2-in (5-cm) lengths
3 tablespoons hoisin sauce
¼ cup (2 fl oz/60 ml) chicken broth mixed with 1 teaspoon cornstarch (cornflour)

Heat 6 cups (48 fl oz/1.5 L) oil in wok until it reaches 375°F (190°C) on deep-frying thermometer or until small bread cube dropped in oil sizzles and turns golden. Working in small batches, add noodles and fry until golden and crisp, 1–2 minutes. Using slotted spoon, remove from oil and drain on paper towels.

In wok over medium–high heat, warm 2 tablespoons vegetable oil. Add garlic, ginger and onion and stir-fry until onion softens slightly, about 3 minutes. Add chicken and stir-fry until browned, 3–4 minutes. Add bell peppers and choy sum or spinach and stir-fry until tender-crisp, about 2 minutes. Stir in hoisin sauce and broth and cornstarch mixture and cook until sauce boils and thickens slightly, about 2 minutes.

To serve, arrange crisp noodles in nest on serving plates. Top with chicken and vegetables.

Chili chicken and vegetables

Serves 4–6
2 tablespoons peanut oil
1 small red chili pepper, seeded and finely chopped
5 oz (150 g) skinless chicken breast or thigh fillet, cut into 1-in (2.5-cm) cubes
6 asparagus spears, cut into 1¼-in (3-cm) pieces
1 bunch bok choy, trimmed and large leaves halved
4 oz (125 g) sugar snap peas or snow peas (mange-touts), trimmed
4 oz (125 g) shiitake mushrooms, sliced
¼ cup (2 fl oz/60 ml) chicken broth
2 teaspoons soy sauce
1 tablespoon rice wine
1 teaspoon Asian sesame oil
crisp fried egg noodles for serving (optional)

In wok over medium heat, warm peanut oil. Add chili pepper and chicken and stir-fry until chicken is golden, 4–5 minutes. Raise heat to medium–high, add asparagus, bok choy, sugar snap peas or snow peas and mushrooms and stir-fry until vegetables soften slightly, 3–4 minutes.

In small bowl, stir together broth, soy sauce, rice wine and sesame oil. Add to wok, reduce heat to medium and cook until heated through.

Serve hot, with crisp fried egg noodles if desired.

Deep-fried chicken wings

Serves 3 or 4
2 teaspoons ground turmeric
1 teaspoon ground chili
2 teaspoons ground cilantro (coriander)
2 teaspoons ground cumin
3 cloves garlic, crushed
12 chicken wings
4 cups (32 fl oz/1 L) vegetable oil for deep frying
Thai sweet chili sauce and lime wedges for serving

In small bowl, combine turmeric, chili, coriander, cumin and garlic. Using hands, rub spices into skin of each chicken wing. Cover and refrigerate for 2 hours.

Heat oil in wok until it reaches 375°F (190°C) on deep-frying thermometer or until small bread cube dropped in oil sizzles and turns golden. Working with one or two wings at a time, add to hot oil and deep-fry until golden brown, 3–4 minutes. Using slotted spoon, remove from wok and drain on paper towels. Keep warm while frying remaining wings.

Serve hot, accompanied with Thai sweet chili sauce for dipping and lime wedges.

Duck with long beans

Serves 4

1 Chinese roast duck
2 teaspoons vegetable oil
4 scallions (shallots/spring onions), chopped
1 tablespoon peeled and shredded fresh ginger
8 long beans, cut into 2½-in (6-cm) lengths
2 tablespoons shredded orange zest
2 tablespoons mirin
1½ tablespoons light soy sauce
steamed white rice for serving

Cut duck into serving pieces, leaving flesh on bone. Set aside. In wok over medium–high heat, warm vegetable oil. Add scallions and ginger and stir-fry until softened, about 2 minutes. Add beans, orange zest, duck, mirin and soy sauce and stir-fry until heated through, 3–4 minutes.

Serve hot, accompanied with steamed white rice.

Crispy wontons with duck

Serves 4

10 scallions (shallots/spring onions), pale portion only, cut into 2-in (5-cm) pieces
2 carrots, peeled and julienned
1 Chinese roast duck
6 cups (48 fl oz/1.5 L) vegetable oil for deep-frying
16 wonton wrappers
½ cup (4 fl oz/125 ml) hoisin sauce

Using sharp knife or scissors, make ¼-in (6-mm) cuts into ends of each scallion piece to make fringe. Place scallions and carrots in bowl of ice water. Refrigerate until scallions curl, about 15 minutes.

Remove meat and skin from duck and coarsely chop; discard skin if desired. Heat oil in wok until it reaches 375°F (190°C) on deep-frying thermometer or

until small bread cube dropped in oil sizzles and turns golden. Working with one wonton at a time and using two sets of tongs, hold wonton in taco shape and lower into oil. Continue to hold wonton until golden and crisp, about 1 minute. Drain on paper towels. Repeat with remaining wontons.

To serve, fill wontons with scallions, carrots and duck. Drizzle with hoisin sauce and serve immediately.

Vegetables

Black-eyed pea and sugar snap stir-fry

Serves 4

1 cup (6½ oz/200 g) dried black-eyed peas (beans)
2 red onions, sliced
juice from 2 lemons
1 tablespoon vegetable oil
2 teaspoons Asian sesame oil
5 oz (150 g) sugar snap peas or snow peas (mange-touts), trimmed
½ cup (2 oz/60 g) chopped scallions (shallots/spring onions)
1 cup (1 oz/30 g) mint leaves
½ cup (¾ oz/20 g) snipped chives
1 teaspoon fish sauce
1 teaspoon light soy sauce

Place black-eyed peas in large bowl, add cold water to cover, cover and allow to stand overnight. Drain and rinse peas and place in saucepan with plenty of water to cover. Bring to boil, reduce heat to low and simmer, uncovered, until tender, about 1 hour. Drain and allow to cool completely.

In bowl, combine onions and lemon juice, cover and allow to stand for 1 hour.

In wok over medium–high heat, warm vegetable and sesame oils. Add sugar snap peas or snow peas and stir-fry until tender-crisp, about 2 minutes. Remove from heat and allow to cool completely. Add black-eyed peas and sugar snap peas or snow peas to bowl with onions. Add scallions, mint, chives, fish sauce and soy sauce. Mix well, cover and refrigerate for 30 minutes. Serve chilled.

Tofu and vegetable stir-fry

Serves 4

¹⁄₃ cup (3 fl oz/90 ml) vegetable oil
6¹⁄₂ oz (200 g) firm tofu, cut into 1-in (2.5-cm) cubes
3 cloves garlic, crushed
2 teaspoons peeled and grated fresh ginger
2 onions, cut into eighths
1 bunch Chinese broccoli, trimmed and cut into 1¹⁄₂-in (4-cm) lengths
3¹⁄₂ oz (105 g) snow peas (mange-touts), trimmed and sliced crosswise
1 red bell pepper (capsicum), seeded and sliced
1 cup (6 oz/180 g) drained canned baby corn
1 bunch bok choy, trimmed and cut into 1¹⁄₂-in (4-cm) lengths,
or 1 bunch spinach, trimmed
2 tablespoons oyster sauce
1 tablespoon light soy sauce
steamed white rice for serving

In wok over medium heat, warm vegetable oil. Working in batches, add tofu and stir-fry until golden on all sides, 2–3 minutes. Using slotted spoon, remove from wok and drain on paper towels. Pour off all but 2 tablespoons oil from wok and return to medium heat. Add garlic, ginger and onions and stir-fry until softened, 2–3 minutes. Add broccoli, snow peas, bell pepper, corn and bok choy or spinach. Stir-fry until vegetables are tender-crisp, 3–4 minutes. Add tofu and oyster and soy sauces and gently stir-fry until heated through, 1–2 minutes.

Serve hot, accompanied with steamed white rice.

Bell peppers and mushrooms with noodles

Serves 4

5 oz (150 g) fresh egg noodles
6 Chinese dried mushrooms
1 tablespoon vegetable oil
1 teaspoon Asian sesame oil
1 red bell pepper (capsicum), seeded and sliced
1 yellow bell pepper (capsicum), seeded and sliced
1 cup (4 oz/125 g) fresh bean sprouts

4 oz (125 g) fresh shiitake mushrooms, sliced
4 oz (125 g) fresh oyster mushrooms, sliced if large
¼ cup (2 fl oz/60 ml) Thai sweet chili sauce
1 tablespoon light soy sauce
¼ cup (¼ oz/7 g) fresh cilantro (fresh coriander) leaves

Bring saucepan of water to boil. Add noodles and cook until tender, about 3 minutes. Drain and set aside.

Place dried mushrooms in small bowl, add boiling water to cover and allow to stand until softened, 10–15 minutes. Drain and squeeze out excess liquid. Thinly slice mushrooms, discarding thick stems.

In wok over medium heat, warm vegetable and sesame oils. Add bell peppers, bean sprouts and fresh mushrooms and stir-fry until slightly softened, 1–2 minutes. Add noodles, reconstituted mushrooms and chili and soy sauces and stir-fry until heated through, 2–3 minutes.

Serve hot, garnished with cilantro leaves.

Desserts

Polenta pudding with mango sauce

Makes 6

½ cup (4 oz/125 g) butter
⅔ cup (5 oz/150 g) sugar
2 teaspoons grated lemon zest
2 eggs
1 cup (5 oz/150 g) self-rising flour
½ teaspoon baking powder
¼ teaspoon salt

⅔ cup (3½ oz/105 g) polenta
½ cup (4 fl oz/125 ml) sour cream
⅓ cup (3 fl oz/90 ml) milk
2 mangos, peeled, pitted and sliced
2 tablespoons confectioners' (icing) sugar
2 tablespoons lime juice
1 teaspoon grated lime zest

Butter six ½ cup (4 fl oz/125 ml) ramekins and line bottoms with parchment (baking) paper. Set aside.

To make puddings, place butter, sugar and lemon zest in bowl. Using electric mixer, beat until light and creamy, 3–4 minutes. Add eggs, one at a time, beating well after each addition. If mixture begins to curdle, add 1 tablespoon all-purpose (plain) flour.

Sift flour, baking powder and salt into bowl. Stir in polenta. Combine sour cream and milk. Fold flour mixture into egg mixture alternately with sour cream mixture. Mix well.

Spoon pudding into prepared ramekins. Cover each with piece of buttered parchment paper. Half fill wok with water (steamer should not touch water) and bring water to boil. Arrange ramekins in steamer, cover and place steamer over boiling water. Steam until puddings are firm to touch, 45–50 minutes. Add more water to wok when necessary.

To make mango sauce, place mangos, sugar and lime juice and zest in food processor. Process until smooth.

Remove steamer from wok and carefully remove ramekins from steamer. Run sharp knife around sides of each ramekin. Invert onto plate and unmold puddings. Serve warm with mango sauce.

Rose water doughnuts

Makes 30 doughnuts
YOGURT SAUCE
6½ oz (200 g) plain (natural) yogurt
3 teaspoons rose water for yogurt sauce,
   plus 2 teaspoons for doughnut mixture
1 tablespoon confectioners' (icing)
   sugar, sifted
DOUGHNUTS
2¼ cups (11 oz/330 g) self-rising flour,
   sifted

½ cup (2 oz/60 g) ground almonds
⅓ cup (3 oz/90 g) butter or ghee, plus
   2 cups (16 fl oz/500 ml) vegetable
   oil or ghee for deep-frying
⅓ cup (3 fl oz/90 ml) plain (natural)
   yogurt
¼ cup (2 fl oz/60 ml) warm water
grated zest of 1 orange
⅓ cup (2½ oz/75 g) superfine (caster)
   sugar

To make yogurt sauce, in a small bowl, combine 6½ oz (200 g) yogurt, 3 teaspoons rose water and confectioners' sugar. Mix well. Cover and refrigerate until ready to serve

In a bowl, combine flour and almonds. Using fingertips, rub ⅓ cup (3 oz/90 g) butter or ghee into flour. Stir in yogurt, warm water, 2 teaspoons rose water and orange zest. Mix to form soft dough. Turn out onto floured work surface. Knead until smooth, about 2 minutes. Divide dough into 30 pieces. Roll each into ball.

Heat 2 cups (16 fl oz/500 ml) vegetable oil or ghee in wok until it reaches 375°F (190°C) on deep-frying thermometer or until small bread cube dropped into liquid sizzles and turns golden. Working in batches, add doughnuts and deep-fry until golden, 5–6 minutes. Using slotted spoon, remove from wok and drain on paper towels. Place superfine sugar on plate and roll each doughnut in sugar until well coated. Serve warm with yogurt sauce.

Spicy fruit salad

Serves 4

1¼ cups (10 fl oz/300 ml) water

½ cup (4 oz/125 g) decorating (crystal) sugar

juice and zest of 1 orange

3 star anise

6 whole black peppercorns

6 whole cardamom pods

3 cinnamon sticks

3 peaches, peeled, pitted and sliced

4 fresh figs, quartered

1½ cups (6½ oz/200 g) blueberries

2 oranges, peeled and cut into segments

Combine water, sugar, orange zest and juice, star anise, peppercorns, cardamom and cinnamon in wok. Place over low heat and stir until sugar dissolves.

Raise heat to medium and bring to boil. Reduce heat to low and simmer, uncovered, for 10 minutes. Remove from heat. Add peaches, figs, blueberries and oranges. Allow to cool to room temperature and serve, or refrigerate for 30 minutes and serve chilled.

Glossary

ASIAN SESAME OIL Oil with a nutty flavor extracted from sesame seeds.

BAMBOO SHOOTS Young shoots of a plant with a mildly sweet flavor and crunchy texture. Boiled before use. Available canned, packed in water.

BOK CHOY Asian variety of cabbage with thick white stalks and mild-flavored dark green leaves. Also known as Chinese cabbage. If unavailable, use Chinese broccoli or choy sum.

CELLOPHANE NOODLES Thin translucent noodles made from mung bean starch. Also called bean thread noodles.

CHINESE BARBECUE PORK Boneless pork marinated in Chinese five-spice powder and soy sauce, then roasted. Sold in slices or strips in Chinese markets. Stores for up to 2 days in refrigerator.

CHINESE BROCCOLI Bitter-tasting broccoli with white flowers. Also known as gai laan. Chinese broccoli can be used in place of choy sum.

CHINESE DRIED MUSHROOMS Intensely flavorful, dark mushrooms that need to be rehydrated before use.

CHINESE ROAST DUCK Sold freshly roasted in Chinese markets. Use 1–2 days after purchase. Substitute roast chicken if unavailable.

CHOY SUM Popular and widely available Chinese green with yellow flowers and thin stalks. Also known as flowering cabbage.

CURRY PASTE Condiment of curry seasonings and red or green chili peppers. Both red curry paste and green curry paste are available bottled. Store in refrigerator after opening.

FISH SAUCE Pungent sauce of salted fermented fish and other seasonings. Products vary in intensity depending on the country of origin.

GARAM MASALA Hot to mild mixture of ground spices used widely in Indian cooking. Often includes cinnamon, black pepper, coriander, cumin, cardamom, cloves and nutmeg.

GHEE Butter from which milk solids have been removed. Gives a rich, buttery taste to curries.

GLUTINOUS RICE Generally white and sometimes dark rice that cooks to a sticky mass rather than separate grains. Also called sticky rice.

HOISIN SAUCE Sweet, thick Chinese sauce made from soybeans and also containing vinegar, sugar, chili peppers and other seasonings.

HOT BEAN PASTE Hot, thick, red-brown sauce made from fermented soybeans, chili peppers, garlic and spices. Also called red bean or chili bean paste.

JASMINE RICE Aromatic long-grain rice popular in Thai cooking.

KAFFIR LIME LEAVES Leaves from the kaffir lime tree generally used dried but also fresh to add an enticing citrus flavor and aroma.

LEMONGRASS Tropical grass with pale stalks with an intense lemon flavor. Wrap in a damp kitchen towel, and store in refrigerator for up to 1 month. Substitute lemon zest if unavailable.

LONG BEAN Also called yard-long bean. Thin, flexible but firm-textured beans cut into short lengths before cooking.

MIRIN Sweet alcoholic wine made from rice. Sweet sherry can be substituted.

MISO Thick paste of fermented ground soybeans. Light-colored ones are milder in flavor than dark-colored pastes.

OYSTER MUSHROOMS Creamy white mushrooms with fan-shaped caps with a mild flavor. Substitute with button mushrooms if unavailable.

OYSTER SAUCE Thick, dark brown Chinese sauce made from fermented dried oysters and soy sauce with an intense or mild briny flavor.

PALM SUGAR Dense, heavy, dark cakes made from the sap of palm trees and sold in Asian markets. Substitute brown sugar if unavailable.

RICE VINEGAR Mildly piquant vinegar made from fermented rice.

RICE WINE Sweet, low-alcohol Chinese wine, also known as shaoxing wine or shaoxing yellow rice wine. Sake or dry sherry can be substituted.

SAMBAL OELEK Spicy Indonesian paste of ground chili peppers combined with salt and occasionally vinegar. It can be used instead of fresh chili peppers.

SHIITAKE MUSHROOMS Meaty mushrooms with light or dark brown caps. Dried shiitakes, also available, need to be rehydrated. Soak, off heat, in boiling water for 10–15 minutes and squeeze dry before slicing or chopping.

SHRIMP PASTE Dried, salted, ground shrimp with a pungent flavor; formed into blocks or cakes.

SOY SAUCE Salty sauce made from fermented soybeans and usually wheat. Dark soy sauce is thicker and often less salty than light soy sauce.

STRAW MUSHROOMS Small mushrooms with round caps and no stems. Available canned, packed in water.

UDON NOODLES Soft, creamy white, Japanese wheat noodles, either fresh or dried and in a variety of widths.

WATER CHESTNUT Tuber of a plant with subtly sweet, crunchy, light-colored flesh. Widely available canned. Store after opening in clean water in the refrigerator for up to 3 weeks. Also known as horses' hooves.

WONTON WRAPPER Thin sheets of fresh or frozen wheat-based or egg-based dough. Also called wonton skins.

Index

INDEX

Cover picture: Pork and nectarine stir-fry, page 42
Pictured on page 2: Rose water doughnuts, page 58
Pictured on page 4: Cilantro shrimp toasts, page 16

A LANSDOWNE BOOK

Published by Apple Press
Sheridan House
4th Floor
112-116 Western Road
Hove
East Sussex BN3 1DD UK

Created and produced by Lansdowne Publishing
Text: Vicki Liley
Photographer: Louise Lister
Stylist: Vicki Liley
Designer: Avril Makula
Editor: Joanne Holliman
Production Manager: Sally Stokes
Project Coordinator: Kate Merrifield

ISBN 1 84092 427 6

Set in Trade Gothic, Journal Text, Gill Sans and Neuropol on QuarkXPress
Printed in Singapore by Kyodo Printing Pte Ltd